Gallery Books
Editor Peter Fallon

AN AUTUMN WIND

Derek Mahon

AN AUTUMN WIND

Gallery Books

An Autumn Wind
is first published
simultaneously in paperback
and in a clothbound edition
on 26 March 2010.

The Gallery Press
Loughcrew
Oldcastle
County Meath
Ireland

www.gallerypress.com

*All rights reserved. For permission
to reprint or broadcast these poems,
write to The Gallery Press.*

© Derek Mahon 2010

ISBN 978 1 85235 486 2 *paperback*
      978 1 85235 487 9 *clothbound*

A CIP catalogue record for this book
is available from the British Library.

Contents

for Rosie FitzGerald Cargin
and family

'A Distant Echo', 'A Country Kitchen' and 'A Quiet Cottage' were published first as broadsides in limited editions by The Gallery Press on the occasions of John Montague's, Seamus Heaney's and Michael Longley's birthdays in 2009. They also appeared in *The Irish Times*.

Other poems were published first in the following periodicals: the *Irish Examiner, The New Yorker* and the *TLS*.

PART ONE

Ithaca

As promised, the Corfu crew put him ashore
at dawn, still dozing, where the sea's roar
turned in his ears, and so he woke at last
on his own soil. Athene threw a sea mist
over the rocks, and after many a year
he didn't know his native earth at first.
'Oh, not *another* island!', he complained.
'Whose meadows are those above the strand?
Will they be primitive and barbarian
or civilized people who will take me in?
Those damn swindlers offered a clear run
to Ithaca, and instead they've set me down
in a strange place I never saw before.'
So musing, lost and bored but still alive,
he gathered up the gear and made his way
along the cold edge of the hissing sea,
up sandy paths, past lemon and wild olive.
'Sir,' said Athene of the shining eyes,
'you must be far gone not to recognize
a famous country known to east and west,
from where the sun rises to where it sets.
It boasts fine pasture for cows and goats,
oak, pine and boatyards. It's not vast,
as you will see, but rich in crops and wine
and generously fed with dew and rain.
I always knew you'd make it in the end —
and here you are, although without your men.
Yes, this is Ithaca, and there's the shrine
to your belovèd wood nymphs.' The sea mist
cleared, and the countryside lay all around.
Astonished at the sight of his own island
— 'Ithaca!' — he raised a pious hand
and spoke to the familiar shrine: 'Receive
my prayer, a prayer of gratitude and love.
I will bring gifts again as in the past

if great Athene lets me live to taste
the joys of home, relinquished years ago,
and sit down with my family once more.'
'Our first task,' said Athene, 'is to stow
your gold and bronzes in the sacred cave
and then decide on where we go from there.'

Blueprint

The gardeners are already waiting.
                                        — Brecht

Trucks from New Jersey (fruit and veg),
panting beneath the window ledge
and drowning out the twitter-cheep
of sparrows on the fire escape,
start up the mad Manhattan day.
The sun, coming the other way,
glitters on offices and planes,
on Jeep, Dodge and commuter trains

streaming from bridge and tunnel mouth,
from out of town, from north and south.
At shark time in the market, though,
some slacker on the Hudson piers
or quiet, tree-lined avenue,
inactive at mid-morning, hears
a different music of the spheres
from what the corporate buzzards know.

There *was* a blueprint from the past
but scribbled on by guilty pens
till it was virtually effaced.
Now, slowly running down despite
what the best economic brains
devise, the culture's clinging tight
to its 'full-spectrum dominance' —
friend and destroyer, both at once.

'Clearance Sale', 'Everything Must Go':
with homeless folks and unemployed
growing in number day and night,
the gritty streets begin to look
as they did eighty years ago

in the old pictures; and it took
another war to put that right
and start us on the upward slide.

Out there in a great plain or wood
a leaf unfolds the rolling news
mutation writes, and the wind sighs
secrets the ancients understood.
Enough, already, with the failed
agendas; give the Algonquin back
the shiny vein of ore we struck
and watch them re-enchant the world!

A Quiet Spot

We tire of cities in the end:
the whirr and blur of it, so long your friend,
grow repetitious and you start to choke
on signage, carbon monoxide, the hard look.
You always knew it would come down
to a dozy seaside town —

not really in the country, no,
but within reach of the countryside,
somewhere alive to season, wind and tide,
far field and wind farm. 'Wrong life,' said Adorno,
'can't be lived rightly.' The right place
is a quiet spot like this

where an expanding river spills,
still trout-rich, from the dewy hills
of Cork, still fertile in a morning mist.
So, do you pause to congratulate yourself
out here at the continental shelf,
far from the hysteria,

on the perfect work-life balancing act
you've found after so many a fugitive year
of travel? If so, let the pause be brief.
Gaia demands your love, the patient earth
your airy sneakers tread expects
humility and care.

It's time now to go back at last
beyond irony and slick depreciation,
past hedge and fencing to a clearer vision,
time to create a future from the past,
tune out the babbling radio waves
and listen to the leaves.

The Thunder Shower

A blink of lightning, then
a rumour, a grumble of white rain
growing in volume, rustling over the ground,
drenching the gravel in a wash of sound.
Drops tap like timpani or shine
like quavers on a line.

It rings on exposed tin,
a suite for water, wind and bin,
plinky Poulenc or strongly groaning Brahms'
rain-strings, a whole string section that describes
the very shapes of thought in warm
self-referential vibes

and spreading ripples. Soon
the whispering roar is a recital.
Jostling rain-crowds, clamorous and vital,
struggle in runnels through the afternoon.
The rhythm becomes a regular beat;
steam rises, body heat —

and now there's city noise,
bits of recorded pop and rock,
the drums, the strident electronic shock,
a vast polyphony, the dense refrain
of wailing siren, truck and train
and incoherent cries.

All human life is there
in the unconfined, continuous crash
whose slow, diffused implosions gather up
car radios and alarms, the honk and beep,
and tiny voices in a crèche
piercing the muggy air.

Squalor and decadence,
the rackety global-franchise rush,
oil wars and water wars, the diatonic
crescendo of a cascading world economy
are audible in the hectic thrash
of this luxurious cadence.

The voice of Baal explodes,
raging and rumbling round the clouds,
frantic to crush the self-sufficient spaces
and re-impose his failed hegemony
in Canaan before moving on
to other simpler places.

At length the twining chords
run thin, a watery sun shines out,
the deluge slowly ceases, the guttural chant
subsides; a thrush sings, and discordant thirds
diminish like an exhausted concert
on the subdominant.

The angry downpour swarms
growling to far-flung fields and farms.
The drains are still alive with trickling water,
a few last drops drip from a broken gutter;
but the storm that created so much fuss
has lost interest in us.

New Space

Swept and scrubbed, the studio fills
with cut cloth, illustrated books,
materials shaped by polished skills
in a time-honoured fashion, one
that aims for a real thing well done
with real significance. Just look

at how green light and shadow fall
on the interior, jug and bowl,
still life, *nature morte*. The place
itself is a still life restored
to living matter, a new space
whose true life is renewed once more.

A coach-house in equestrian days,
it makes one with the vegetable
garden beyond the ceramic glaze
inside and the converted stable
loft where an old record plays
to pram and pine and summer breeze.

It's all the one, the clay, the cloth,
art, music and organic growth
nursing the venerable ideal
of spirit lodged within the real.
Tolstoy, who later disapproved
of operas, plays and novels, loved

doorknobs, utensils, toys and song,
the homespun that the peasants wore —
anything simple, strong and clean,
art that was modest, not a chore;
and rhyming verses, not too long,
that say exactly what they mean.

Though the sun rises in a blaze
these mornings, breaking up the haze,
I'm less in love with the sublime,
more interested in the neat rows
laid out to raise the beans and peas,
rosemary, parsley, sage and thyme.

The weight of a bone-handled knife
signifies more in human life
than our aesthetics ever can;
form follows function. Once again
we look to the still living whole
to heal the heart and cure the soul.

Air India

(Delhi-Heathrow)

A haughty camel train in the rush hour,
a holy cow chewing a cardboard box,
sand-thudding fruit, a dusty star —
these are the images that recur,
and the new office blocks.

Sand-scraping branches making *namaskar*
to the brown sea from a 'Bounty'-wrapper beach,
a nipper's goofy toy inflatable shark,
idle kites circling a railway bridge,
old Delhi after dark;

a woodsmoke evening, the pink architecture,
moth-fluttering crowds around the sanctuary
where six-branched Shiva sits like a gilt candlestick,
some hunched-up creature watching
the sunrise from a cedar tree . . .
But the clearest picture

is a weed-trailing yard of wood and brick
up a dim lane behind a bicycle shop
with a quick monkey, rhesus or macaque,
clinging for dear life to a water pipe,
the slowly dripping tap.

World Trade Talks

Downturn Means CO$_2$ Targets Now Achievable

A 'Hindu' growth rate,
hedges against the winds
of double-edged finance; organic crops
and comely maidens, is it too late
to push for these demands
and pious hopes?

The great Naomi Klein
condemns, in *The Shock Doctrine*,
the Chicago Boys, the World Bank and the IMF,
the dirty tricks and genocidal mischief
inflicted upon the weak
who now fight back.

A hare in the corn
scared by the war machine
and cornered trembling in its exposed acre,
a sacred thing projected on the moon
when the full moon is clear,
survives the roar

by lying low
in the heart-withering breeze.
Next spring, when a new crop begins to grow,
let it not be genetically modified
but such as the ancients sowed
in the old days.

Ash and Aspen

Their captive spirits groan as one
with a new yearning to be free
of the old fate, the old constraints —
faint whispers of conspiracy
from hazel, juniper and birch
shaking arthritic finger joints,
keening together each alone
in unison. Which witch is which?

Wide, oval mouths of agèd ash
vowel their bondage; stricken hands
and keys articulate their anguish.
They are committed root and branch
and dream of flight to no avail,
shrinking to rigid furniture,
table and wardrobe, desk and chair,
everything 'Antaeus-like'. Meanwhile

the aspen whistles fast and loud
with forecast and astonishment,
light heart and breezy equinoxes.
Oceans rustle in the strings
of this celestial instrument.
Its shiny paper pours like wings
of inspiration; the soft wood
is used for matches and matchboxes.

Growth

The gardens have survived the ice
that laid the country bare and clear,
their grasses rising fast and fierce
through splintered water, frosty air,
soft swords reclaiming heritage
from squeaking mud and creaking ditch.

After the dawn commuters leave
in the Range Rovers, four by four,
the quiet of an hour's reprieve
except on a few building sites.
The global oil-price crisis bites;
an April mist lifts from the shore.

Not 'rock and thorn' but field and wood
slope to the sea below the town.
The tree stands where it always stood,
a knuckly oak beside the spring
reaching skywards like a Druid,
firm in its place and flourishing.

The secret source still running clean
of brick dust and detergent froth
that wither so much natural growth,
the woodpigeon, the thrush and wren
hide in the branches to discharge
soul music to the world at large.

Quercus petraea, Dair ghaelach —
sunlight smokes in its archaic
antlers and visceral mistletoe.
Old oak of Durrow and Kildare!
The leaves reflect a golden glow;
no lightning strike has crackled there.

The Seasons

for Matthew Geden

I

Day-stars like daisies on a field of sky.
The nuclear subs are keeping sinister watch
while sun heat focuses on the cabbage patch.
What weird weather can we expect this July?
Tornado, hail, some sort of freak tempest?
The bonfire month, *and another storm brewing:*
I hear it sing i' th' wind, and among the leaves.
But out here in the hot pastures of the west,
no Google goggling at our marginal lives,
there are still corners where a lark can sing.

2

We prospered and made hay while the sun shone.
Now autumn skies, yellow and grey, sow rain
on summer debris, *Ambre Solaire*, crushed bracken,
we clear the dead leaves from a blocked drain
and tap barometers since the weather's taken
a sudden turn for the worse. Contentious crows
congregate of an evening at St Multose';
the harvest hymns float out from Gothic windows
on Maersk, docked sailing-boats and guesthouses
closed for the winter now the guests have gone.

3

The reading period, and on the writing desk
quarto and lamplight in the early dusk.
If we don't travel now we hibernate
with other locals at the Tap Tavern
beside an open hearth, our winter haven.

Glowing cinders nuzzle the warm grate
while outside, ghostly in a starlit street,
creaking signs and a novelistic breeze.
Urgent footsteps fade into the night
leaving us to our pub talk and reveries.

4

A fly-dazzling disc in the open door,
hung on a ribbon, catches light and blinks
as the sun spokes on gardens and seascapes,
drawing up dew, exposing hidden depths,
old shipwrecks visible from the air. A northern
draught blows flower scents to the blue horizon;
a yawl, Bermuda-rigged, shakes out its linen
watched by the yachties, blow-ins, quiet drunks
and the new girls with parasols in their drinks.
Springs gush in a shower of flowering hawthorn.

After the Storm

After the storm a tentative blackbird chorus,
silent throughout it, started cheeping again.
The city, for fear of a worse overflow,
had unlocked dams, so water levels rose
at an alarming rate; the rivers burst
their banks, swamping fields in a sea of rain,
and flooded low-lying districts in one go,
the waters sparing neither man nor beast.
Square miles shrank as a sudden deluge rushed
from the rain-sodden hills. *Ye nymphes of Bandon*,
where were you when the great south-facing windows
of heaven were opened and it bucketed down
on quiet Munster? No one had imagined
embankments would give way under the surge,
the River Lee engulfing market towns'
water mains, drains and residential lanes.
It struck in late November, so by and large
no ripening crops suffered, no standing grain,
but haylofts were awash and much of the hard
work of the summer proved to be in vain.
Reservoirs, lakes poured down in a tide of mud
submerging farms. An astonishing six inches
fell in a single night from inky cloud.
Not much distinction now between sea and land:
some sat in dinghies rowing where they'd sown,
navigating their own depth-refracted ground
and scaring salmon from among the branches.
Global warming, of course, but more like war
as if dam-busting bombers had been here:
aerial photographs of the worst-hit areas
showed roads, bridges, basic infrastructure
devastated, the kind of thing you expect
in China or Louisiana but not in Cork.
Detritus of the years, carpet and car,
computers and a wide range of expensive

gadgetry went spinning down the river
with furniture and linen, crockery, shoes
and clothes, until it finally gave over;
not everyone had full insurance cover.
The inquiry dealt only with technical issues,
avoiding larger questions. Telephone
lines down, 'Boil Water' notices in force,
drainage schemes overwhelmed and of no use,
authorities hinted that it could've been worse.
(There would be building work for months to come,
developers would have no cause to complain.)
A general cleaning-up operation began;
houses, garages, skips gleamed with the slime
deposited everywhere like a disease.
We will get over it though we're not sure how.
The country sighed in the calm after the storm,
emergency services got to grips with the grim
sequel as drowned townlands emerged at last,
the earth increasing as the flow decreased.
The birds, crowing and piping with relief,
announced a partial return to normal life
and light shone in the cloud until next time.
It's snow and black ice we've to contend with now.

Beached Whale

Snow from the north, hail, and a ruffled gull
rises from cold dunes at break of day
when the shore belongs to the gale,
the frozen algae and the beached whale
fluke-thrashing as she breathes her dying
breaths and gradually subsides
under the great weight of her own insides.

The transatlantic dash was nothing to her,
a fine finback, her notion of a trip
some new dimension, gravity defied,
the dive at dusk through the empyrean
whooping and chuckling in her slick and drip,
stinking and scooping up the fry,
rusty and barnacled like an old steamship.

On moonlit nights her bubbling orifices
dribbled for miles, mysterious and capricious,
where she went spouting, eerie as Moby Dick,
far from the known sea-lanes, her whistle and click
distinguishable from Cape Clear to Cape Race;
on a calm day she'd snooze
exposed and ruminant on the sunny surface.

Out of her depth now, her rorqual pleats
ivory fading to grey as the tide retreats,
her brain at rest, with her huge size
she has admirers in her drowsy eyes —
surfers and tourists, children, families
who never saw a whale before;
and the news cameras, RTÉ, Channel 4.

A tired eye closes after so many years,
so much experience, travel, league upon league
of ocean, wild sunrises and sunsets,

tropical storms, long vistas, wind and stars;
and she gives up the ghost
not in the unfathomable dark forest
of sea, but here on the strand at Timoleague.

Pliny thought dolphins beached for love of man,
aspiring to human life. A mighty beast
like this has other reasons (pheromone,
exhaustion, age), yet when she gasps her last
bad breath on the glassy sand she gives
her body to flensing knives
and the flesh falls away in heavy leaves —

source once of lamp oil, glue and candle grease.
Dead of some strange respiratory disease,
reduced to the rib-cage of an old wreck,
entrails strewn on mud, the stomach
stripped and the organs — heart, liver
and lights — retrieved for research,
she knows we aim to make a study of her;

to study the cortex, the skin thick and thin,
her ancient knowledge of the seas and rocks
we left to climb up on the burning shore
and still revisit in dreams and sex,
where the soft human paw
has the reflex of an unthinking fin
or a nerve twitching in primordial depths.

At the Butler Arms

No boats this week, too choppy, so we watch
from a spread table beneath
a Charlie Chaplin photograph
who often came here for a holiday;
or we drive over to Finian's Cove to study
the eight-mile stretch

of water between here and Sceilig Mhichíl
where the old anchorites
and monks who chose the place and raised
a church, two chapels and six drystone huts,
survived on dulse and mackerel
out in the haze.

No pleasant woodland there, no grazing deer
such as the others knew
above fly-bubbling salmon streams ashore
in field and forest beneath oak and yew —
not calm, contemplative ease
but violent seas.

Six hundred years of plainchant and response,
gannet and cormorant; six
centuries of the 'crude bronze crucifix'
in Finian's church, wine cup and canticle,
prayer book and reading candle,
thistles, sea-campions.

How could you get inside their bony heads?
Wrapped up in mystic mists,
they spent the hours and years
wrestling with the hot flesh in their cold beds,
their backs to Europe and the wars,
talking to ghosts.

What news of the great world, of Gaul and Rome,
Iona and Cappadocia? Some,
but late; prostrate at Easter in the nave
they listened to the whistling wave
and saw the sun sink in an infinite ocean
world of its own.

Strong winds continue, so no trip this time.
Still, it could be predictable to climb
to the immense height and the whole shocking
reach of the Atlantic (with special care
since there's no handrail there).
No going back,

is there, to that wild hush of dedication,
to the solitude, the intense belief,
the last rock of an abandoned civilization
whose dim lights glimmered in a distant age
to illuminate at the edge
a future life.

Sceilig Bay

Tomás Rua Ó Súilleabháin, 1785-1848

One fine, soft morning — St Michael's Day —
Communion-bound in the Sceilig Bay,
we watched as the breakers multiplied,
rain threatened and a strong wind blew.
We wisely decided on turning back
and finding harbour beyond Bray Head;
starting up when I heard the crew,
I who'd been dozing was wide awake.

Our seine-boat was a delight that morning,
high in the waves, six oars at work,
the sail full and the rowlocks slick,
every board alive and singing.
We'd held her fast in the flying foam
surging and sparkling beneath the beam;
no stir on the water from here to Dingle
until we made for St Michael's Rock —

when Sow Cliff there on the port side
shrieked fit to be tied, Gull Sound
roared aloud like a bull in pain,
the Groaner groaned in the howling wind.
Thanks be to Jesus we weren't drowned
and stretched in the dark depths of the tide
but spared for another, quieter run
when, please God, we may try again.

The priest prayed loudly in the stern
to spare the boat and save the men,
and he must have been heard in heaven above
as the white wave-crests crashed over us
for we cleared Rincarragh in due course
with the Narrows a flat calm after the sea;

so we kept on till we came to shore
and broached a barrel at Seán Magee's.

God, we were shook, so we sat all night
and emptied the porter, watching the gale
from a warm room until first light
and giving thanks for our lucky escape.
Ribbed, tarred and finished by Seán O'Neill,
that little boat will never know harm:
where would you find a finer ship
to deliver you safe from such a storm?

Synge Dying

I didn't start it exactly but I was among
the first with bike and camera
to visit the wilder shores
of Kerry and Connemara
in search of old reality, stories,
folklore and traditional song.
I even introduced the clock to Aran.

Not real to myself, a sick man fighting for life
in the fey breezes and raw winds,
I was in two minds
about my right to be there
writing up the rough holy ground,
the roads, the *céilí* and the hiring fair.

But there in words I found
the living world I couldn't share;
now from the pillows
my gaze travels
past smoking chimneys to the distant hills.

A Building Site

Exposed dorms and corridors
squeak under the tracks
of cranes and earth-movers
and a fast shower rakes
the shattered greenhouses.

The school, a living surge
of nuns, skirts, blazers
and aprons, saw religion
take wing and fly away;
the site's a *tabula rasa.*

Of the old convent nothing
remains on this dark day.
New people in the prescribed
yellow protective clothing
string razor wire; from one

bare room to the next
the dangling terminals
and boxes of fresh bricks.
Beneath sliding skies
the new flats will rise.

One more dour complaint
at plywood and cement?
Certainly, though of course
perpetual change and flux
are the true element.

A grim summer, but if
fortuitous light strikes
the rubble and a sun-spoke
pierces a cloud rift
the meaning becomes clear.

The deconstruction here
— smashed tiles, splintered
wood, dismantled banisters,
tarpaulin and building gear
where once a convent stood —

opens a special place,
a field of rough energy
suspended for a minute
not at an 'interface'
or even a 'cutting edge'

but at a spinning centre
of heightened consciousness,
gives giddy glimpses into
the universe of blown
dust and distant stars.

This is the great answer
granted at a glance
and rained upon at once,
the magic coalition
of concrete circumstance —

a momentary, oblique
vision of an unknown
eternal dispensation,
the infinite republic
of primary creation.

Autumn Skies

I A DISTANT ECHO

Garvaghey, a 'rough field',
Dungannon and Armagh
remember the O'Neills
before the Tudor armies
trampled bog and sheugh.
We revel in that stuff —

still relevant enough
as our own new century
crushes the wild contours
of the ancestral dream.
Earth-movers champ and cough
at ancient glen and stream.

Same story everywhere,
the old St-Germain
market and Super-Cannes
a corporate nightmare
while a bard holds aloof
under the leaking roof

of a dark house in Schull.
A killer roams the hills
but Muses mind with love
the hierophantic cave.
The *ceol mór* of long ago
lives on as a distant echo

drowned out by the noise
of ambient retail rock;
but a poet makes the soul

that only he can make
in a great singing school
of heather and wild dog rose.

2 A COUNTRY KITCHEN

'Walking into eternity'
along the breathing strand
there's that modality
immediately to hand —
spawn, wrack, far-out sea
and Howth Head beyond.

This is how it begins,
devotion to the real things
of a clean-swept morning:
leaf-drip and birdsong,
work sounds, the rich
air of a country kitchen.

We toy with rhythm and rhyme
at a freshly lit hearth;
from under a close blanket
of ground fog the earth
opens up to a cloudstream
westwards in the Atlantic.

The world of simple fact
gleams with water, yields
to the plough. A gull-race
follows the working tractor.
Quidditas: the used fields
of Ulster and ancient Greece;

and always the same river,
the oracle and universe
with no circumference,
that infinite resource.
If a thing happens once
it happens once for ever.

3 A QUIET COTTAGE

It all began at Inst.
You were among the finest
forwards in the great game
learning from the scrum
how to advance against
the exigencies of form.

'Think globally and act
locally': folk and jazz
sing to the autumn skies
and your creative tact.
Our cultural confusion
worked for resolution.

You found it in a quiet
cottage down the west
and took the answer back
to battered old Belfast;
bubbles of image-smoke
rose from a chimney pot.

Guns under the floorboards,
cooped-up doves and pigeons
grumbled to the back yards

above belovèd motorbikes
in a city of rough politics
and murderous religions —

but the best thoughts survive
decades of fear and hate;
linen, cloud and snow
absorb the blood and sweat.
Now we relax and live
the lives we used to know.

Earth voices in the branches,
butterflies at the flowers
on overgrown trenches,
and recent graves, replace
the historical nightmares.
Now we can die in peace.

Art and Reality

for James Simmons, obiit 20/6/01

Down white empty beaches my voice rang.

Jimmy, the harbour lights still shine
on Kerr St and the railway line
from cold Portrush to cold Coleraine
and so to the great world; cold rain
still hammers into the West Strand
and the faint coast of Donegal,
the 'farther shore', the shining land
of childhood, fun and funeral.

Who would have thought you'd be the first
to quit the uproar of life's feast?
Barry's Amusements still go round;
the old Arcadia where once
the great Dave Glover and his band
played to your youthful innocence
still stands where the Atlantic knocks,
a pleasure dome above the rocks

that lost its neon sign long since.
The gulls still scream there on the roof
as if they miss your voice, as if
disconsolate for the cheery sight
of their blithe poet stepping out
in his trademark tweed overcoat —
a nonchalant rebel, *blasé*, bluff,
constantly singing, born to dance.

Burning the energy, burning up
the roads, not knowing when to stop,
every day was a rave and every
evening a new discovery.

Sworn to our tricky art, you chose
reality over art and pose —
an 'Honest Ulsterman' although
a rogue and romantic even so.

That title always bothered me,
the 'honest' claim seemed to imply
others were charlatans or worse:
we disagreed there at the start
one evening in the Longleys' house.
Perhaps reality and art,
grown disputatious, even thought
the two of them were poles apart

and not the mates they really are.
Oh, you could be a royal pain,
thorn in the side, flea in the ear.
Had you but *spar'd* your *tongue and pen*
you *might have rose like other men* —
though what's the point of 'rising' when
the kind of work we favoured thrives
in the night silence of the nerves?

When the guitars were packed away
and your Resistance Cabaret
took off into the sleeping town
planets and 'gaseous' sky looked down
on a dark province, brick and tile,
with cold indifference: not your style,
but didn't you tell it as it was?
'We're here because we're here because.'

You cherished girls of every age
and pitied the poor Paisleyite
deprived of your advantages.

Often your dodgy sexual ethic
emptied front rows; some splenetic
alderman would throw a tantrum.
Hillsborough, Portadown and Antrim
saw shocked audiences walk out.

We flinch, of course, when someone writes
our story by his different lights;
yet what I say agrees, I know,
with your self-estimate. We two
both wanted to help dissipate
the 'guilt and infantile self-hate',
each in his way, and find a voice
for the strange place bequeathed to us.

The hard men have renounced the gun
on *both* sides, you'd be pleased to hear.
Two kinds of gullibles have begun,
hundreds of years too late, to share
the benefits; though, still unbowed,
we get around our psychic pain
by picking on the immigrant crowd:
we have disgraced ourselves again.

'Love what you can, die game,' you said —
and so you did, and so you did.
Your special genius found release
transporting the sad heart that longs
for new space and an open mind;
then you relinquished the old place
to sing on that white stretch of sand
in the distance. I still hum your songs.

An Aspiring Spirit

after Quevedo

The final dark can take away my eyesight,
obliterating the white blaze of day;
it can release my soul and maybe gratify
the anxious hope of an eternal light —

but even on the farther shore it won't deter
the thought of where my earthly being burned:
blithely ignoring the strict rules, my fond
desire will swim back through the icy water.

The life that held such an aspiring spirit,
the arteries that fed so much impatience,
the marrow once so glisteningly bright

may wither, but their ardour will survive.
There will be ashes, yes, but smouldering ashes;
there will be dust, but dust glowing with love.

Antrim Road

after Baudelaire

I can still see that first suburban house,
whitewashed and tiny, tiny but at peace,
a 'Dresden' figurine next to the clock
holding her skirt out as she reads a book.
A fiery evening sun, intensely hot,
burns at the window from a garden hut,
a curious red eye between two clouds
silently watching mushy peas and spuds,
and throws out long, imposing shadow-shapes
on the white homework and the bottled ships.

Romance

after Rimbaud

1

Nothing is serious when you're seventeen.
One evening, sick of the beer and the lemonade,
the noise and bright lights of the café scene,
you sit out under trees on the promenade.

A scent of lime there in the hot June nights.
The air engulfs you with its summery glow;
not far away the wine fumes and the shouts
float up on a soft breeze from down below.

2

You try to fix your gaze on a patch of blue
framed like a picture in the branchy night
pierced by a star, sharp but dissolving now,
quivering slightly, tiny, perfectly white.

A June night! Seventeen! You're getting drunk.
You sip champagne, the stuff goes to your head;
you wander off, imagining some punk
groupie clinging to you or in your bed.

3

The daft heart drifts to popular romance —
when, suddenly, that nice Charmaine goes by,
delightful in the pale glare of the lamps
under her stuffy father's furious eye.

Since you look interesting, if a little weird,
she throws you an alert and lively glance,

two shoes tickety-boo in the boulevard,
and a soppy song dies on your lips at once.

4

Now you're in love (she giggles at your poem) —
in love, until the holidays are through.
Your pals avoid you, love being 'bad form',
and the next day she grants a rendezvous . . . !

That evening, back to the rowdy café scene,
ordering up the beer and the lemonade.
Nothing is serious when you're seventeen
and lime trees are in leaf on the promenade.

Balcony of Europe

for Aidan and Alannah Higgins

The dictator's portrait dominated the airport
in those days, the first thing you noticed
after the cold police; his arms, a vivid
fistful of forked lightning, blazed
on the bus station and the road north-east
to the olive hills where the novelist lived.
The kitchen tap gave only a dry cough;
it was pitch-black up there with the light off.

Down here at the sea front forty years later,
on the *paseo*, at the Balcón de Europa bar
cameras, recorded accordion and guitar.
No shortage now of light or water,
everything so much brighter and better —
old wounds healed, old bones reconstituted;
and a young one in a swimsuit plays
on the shore as she did in ancient days

when she wasn't only a girl but a creature
of myth, a Phoenician king's abducted daughter
with a white bull between her knees,
borne out to a sun-white sea shaking with fear
and exhilaration far from her shocked sisters,
gripping the horns, clutching the curly hair,
et tremulae sinuantur flamine vestes
('her floaty garments fluttering in the breeze').

Nerja

Under the Volcanoes

Todo se puede corregir.
— César Manrique, 1985

The heat-seekers of Cork have been coming here
to Lanzarote year after solar year
in the high season, to sit on balconies
and bob like cork in the sub-tropical seas.
A cruise ship, bound for Europe, shimmers past
far out, its music system going full blast,
to join October in the temperate zones.
It's hereabouts, said Plato in *Timaeus*,
the lost Atlantis lies; and the Hesperides
retain their charm, even in these dark days.
The golden apples of the sun, of course,
are the great draw, and the rich local wines
uncorked as a red African disc swoons
into the western sea. The charcoal-black
volcanic sand, the cactus thick and coarse
in the dry scrub beyond the beaten track
make this a different kind of destination.
MacNeice chose Iceland for his holiday stuff
as if he couldn't ever get north enough —
but the Cork crowd, weary of fog and rain,
can fly directly to this part of Spain,
to this ferocious, natural work of art,
wind sculpture rising from each roundabout,
an immense, site-specific installation-piece
parque temático; in the Manrique place,
a maker's cave and an obsidian mine
carved from the airy bubbles underground,
his own drawings, Tàpies and Joan Miró,
together with local work, are on permanent show.
The 'house' itself, art or ingenious kitsch
like a caged pontiff or a runny watch?

White-fronted civilization has made a stand
with tiered holiday flats above the sand
and rowdy beach parties on summer nights;
but it's precarious, for just inland
we've basalt rocks, boulders like meteorites
and, under the volcanoes, active furnaces
to remind us of the origins of the arts.
Do we need disaster to bring out the best,
calamity as a necessary precondition?
On 1 September, 1730, the Yaiza parish priest,
like the young Pliny writing from Pompeii,
was startled by a violent detonation,
an avalanche of lava, ash, debris,
a heavy rain of boiling condensation,
red hill-ranges emerging from the earth
and searing dust storms, the great cosmic breath.

Sun worship, water sports; but Lanzarote,
much more than just a paradise for the yachtie
and windsurfer, provides an opportunity
to see things as they were and might be like:
low-lying life tucked into the landscape,
not only 'heritage' but a source of hope,
a civilization built on igneous rock
still cruel to the eye, hot to the touch,
formed from the dark interior of the globe
where cork and honeysuckle start from scratch
at dewfall, in the absence of other noise,
watched over by Nuestra Señora de los Remedios.
Maybe this was the world when it began,
slowly evolving myrtle, laurel, vine,
your backstroke in the white track of the sun;
but it's the old we notice in October —
the retired codger, brown as an almond, studying
the financial pages of the *Herald Tribune*,

sunk in a deckchair in his private dune;
the centenarian slowly wheeled along
the promenade; unhurried couples, sober
and reminiscent, of advancing age,
testing the temperature at the water's edge.

After the holliers, no place for the young.
What irks me now at this end of the season
is wind and limb, cholesterol and gout
de-rhapsodizing the sun-lanced horizon,
the slowdown, with old age starting for real;
a bad back. When we get back to Kinsale
I sit late listening to an autumn wind
shaking the window, blowing leaves about
these northern gardens with an angry sound,
imposing chaos where I try to wring
form from the debris choking up the mind.
The equinoctial gales are overdue,
wind-banging door and moaning chimney flue.
Best practice recommends we let it be,
don't force the issue of formality,
yield to the natural shape on its own ground,
the rock formation; but the ancient rage
for order, the old curse, is too ingrained:
'Everything can be remedied', thyme and sage
redeemed from fire, the most unpromising
material shaped into a living thing
outlasting winter to a temperate spring.

Los Jameos — Kinsale

PART TWO

River of Stars

The Long Road to Sichuan

Li T'ai-Po, 701-762

The long road to Sichuan, so steep and high,
is harder to climb than the road to heaven.
Ts'an Tsung and Yu Fu opened up this region
eight thousand years ago, crossing the Ch'in
border by paths known only to the raven,
and looked west where once the mountains split
and the earth crumpled. Many died; they built
tracks and bridges in a continuous chain
where six dragons rotate around the sun.
Even cranes find it hard to come this way,
the gibbons climb slowly and anxiously.
We scale the Pleiades and grasp Orion;
past rock and cliff we reach the barren moon
exhausted, and stretch out with a long sigh.
When will we ever get back? Jackdaw and crow
croak in the morning to an empty sky.
The long road to Sichuan, so steep and high,
is harder to climb than the road to heaven.
A blasted pine leans over a ravine
where cataracts and rapids boil below
and boulders crash down where we aim to go.
Cheng-du provides some consolation, though
it's nothing to the going-home consolation.
The long road to Sichuan, so steep and high,
is harder to climb than the road to heaven.
I look to east and west with a long sigh.

Cheng-du: Sichuan capital

The War Zone

Li T'ai-Po

Above the Altai Mountains the moon rises
and drifts in a sea of cloud; a desert wind
blows down the valleys for a thousand miles.
The sons of Han march through Manchuria
while Tartars stare down from the Pamirs
at this old war zone where so many died.
Soldiers picture the homes they left behind
where anxious women watch from upper floors.

A Kettle of Wine

Li T'ai-Po

Sitting among flowers with a kettle of wine
I lift my cup and drink to the bright moon.
A party of three: the moon, my shadow and me.
The moon is no drinker, sadly; however
I toast the spring and the spring flowers.
When I sing my shadow bobs in the Yellow River,
when I dance the moonbeams in the water waver.
Sober, we are content here in a group;
when we get drunk my shadow and I break up.
To pledge eternal amity we gather
in cloud depths and in a river of stars.

The Thatched Hut

Ch'iu Wei, 710-775

The road goes up for miles into the mountain
and here at the top is your thatched hut,
but nobody's at home and the door is shut.
Squinting through the window I see a plain
table, a simple chair. You must be out
walking, fishing perhaps. Weaving about
like swifts, we fail to meet. I stand still
in the long grass shining with recent rain
as peace descends, startling the eye and ear
to something like an ecstatic trance.
When it recedes I go back down the hill:
there's no need to wait for you to appear,
I've understood your theory of existence.

A Shabby Welcome

Tu Fu, 712-770

Springtime, pine scent, and the river in spate.
Only the seagulls visit our lonely home.
I realize as I open the garden gate
the path hasn't been swept: a shabby welcome.
So far from town we have no delicacies
and can offer only vegetarian dishes.
As you'd expect, we are too poor for wine
but somewhere I've a drop of old moonshine.

Thinking of Li Po

Tu Fu

Severance caused by death is an end of life
but the lost living are a persistent grief.
No word from you in your harsh banishment
among the malarial swamps beyond Kiang-nan.
I think of the companionship we knew
and summon up your spirit, half afraid
you've vanished into everlasting shade —
but no, you're still alive though never seen,
caught in the web of politics. The moon
shining in through the windows of my house
seems to illuminate your remembered face.
The lakes are fathoms deep, the rivers wide
beneath immeasurable high-sailing cloud,
and breezes chop the Yangtse's rippling surface.
Don't lose the oars that always guided you!
(I've seen you in a dream scratching your old
white head like one forced to renounce his due.)
We still keep our elaborate routine
here in Chang-an; you languish in the cold.
I know your thoughts tonight so far from home,
old friend. I understand: eternal fame
is a poor consolation when life is done.

Chang-an: T'ang capital

Autumn Fields

Tu Fu

The autumn fields grow bleaker every day
and the streams colder as the sky changes.
We're living here in exile at K'uei-chou
among country people on the middle Yangtse.
Others will taste the fruits of my best years.
We cultivate our beans and cabbages;
I eat sparingly now in my old age
and throw our scraps to the local carp.

It's easy to understand the flow of life
where everything fulfils its own nature
with fish happiest in the deepest water
and birds most at home in the leafiest wood;
but worldly ambition is for younger men,
at my age I'm resigned to failing powers.
An autumn wind shivers my walking stick
but peace of mind resides in ferns, flowers,

music and daily habit for equilibrium,
regular exercise to keep up the strength.
I sit in the bamboo sunshine of my library,
a straw hat over my eyes, a student
of wind-blown pine cones, ants and midges,
trivial things we tend to ignore.
On my woodland walks I pause before
the scents of willowherb and water mint.

The sands are shining on the farther shore
and an evening glow crimsons the high ridges.
Slow-pulsing gills surprise the tripping ripples
and tired wings contend with a rising wind.
Sounds of washing come from the little bridges,
woodmen sing as they chop up the dead wood.

It's frosty now, with snow on the dark air;
white drifts will cut us off from the world.

My intention was to shine among the eagles
but it's ducks and geese I'm going down among.
The autumn river is in full spate:
I hear the thundering gorges roar at night.
The upland paths are blocked by strewn rubble
and timber; immense clouds obscure the sun.
My children chatter in the local tongue
and I can't see them prospering in Chang-an.

PART THREE

Raw Material

for Gopal and Amrita Singh

The fictitious Hindi poet Gopal Singh was born in Kashmir in 1959 and lives in Delhi, where for many years he was Arts Editor of the monthly New India. *He has published ten books of verse, most recently* Kcha-Mal *(Raw Material), 2009, from which this is a selection. Singh's is a densely intertextual poetry which frequently references the work of others — Bengalis, Tamils — with the result that it almost reads like a telescopic anthology of the contemporary Indian canon; but his own distinctive voice is unmistakable. He provided literal drafts for these rather free versions and approved the results. I would like to thank him for his help and forbearance (much has been lost in translation); also Ireland Literature Exchange for its support.*

A Child of the Forest

A child of the forest, I roam city slums.
Dinner clatters, the *cuit*, the *cru*;
dhal simmers on cow-dung fires,
samosas fry beneath tangled wires
in a thousand frugal homes.

A shack in the woods and a few
bamboo sticks would do
but I keep coming
back to life
whose blaze darkens the stars.

Tata. Maruti. IndiCom. IndiGo.
Bavinder Ready Cash. Dubai
Is Closer than You Know.
Unwind Beneath the Goa Sky.

The raw stuff of the future
sighs as I drive home
at the cow-dust hour
past twinkling compounds,
building sites
and forests of billboards.

Will I ever outgrow
the babble of words?

New Retina Solutions.
Think Skin. Gitanjali.
Embrace the Spiritual
to Beat the Credit Crunch.

Asphalt Roads

The sun bangs like a gun on Rajasthan,
the sandstone fort, the asphalt road,
the desert. Rain drums in the mud
and flashes like a sword
above the plain;
mists rise like ghosts or scents
from lanes, tanks, palm thatch,
palm and pine.
Time lives in a stagnant pond
that sees cloud best
and a periwinkle sky beyond.

Those who scrape and scratch
a life from the soil watch
the clicking corn seethe,
the rice, the maize
awaiting the quick scythe.

When the monsoon relents
and the opaque past
vanishes, wind rises
and sings to a blind old man
crouched in the luminous dust
where he began,
imagining a future.

Raw Material

The recycling of old shoes
as raw material
makes artwork
of the contingent real
when sunlight,
finding them
among shadows,
throws
shadow shapes on their used souls.

Only material forms die
says the *Gita*,
the dusty soul within
alone survives
even as we discard
one body for another.
Avatar and aviator,
I who was once a virus,
once a mosquito,
begin to re-imagine
my previous lives.

My previous lives were long ago
in Chittagong and Kathmandu
but there is life to come
when we rejoin the dust

or drift downstream
and sink into the sand like foam.

Plant Life

The plants grow audibly at night
whispering amongst themselves
about their private lives,
the wild love in the leaves,
the nectar in the flower,
remembering the clear
spring meadows of Kashmir
and the lost horizons of Tibet.

As they evolve in knowing growth
and time-lapse circumspection
they slowly learn to shun
the shade and find the sun;
but this is not enough.

The flowers want to be tough,
to think and propagate,
escape from the close earth,
the traditional dark fate,
chase space and light
and share the world above.

Dharma Bums

Those who raise their eyes
to the beautiful words
— 'contentment', 'paradise' —
can never . . . *Dharma?*
What do they know
of dharma, these spoilt kids
without warmth, without charm?
Eternity takes time.

They sit like tramps
beside the road,
each on a dusty bum,
when they should be at home
in advertising.

Advertising the benefits
of our spirituality —
Ganesh the god of profit,
Saraswati the celebrant of it,
Rama of many dominions
and Krishna, 'brighter than a thousand suns'.

A New Earth

We hid, heads in a cloud,
till the worst was over.
A perpendicular
rain curtain covered
the nightbound countryside.

As day broke a redstart
chip-chattered to the light
of a new earth on Earth.
Parrot and squirrel
drink from the same bird table;

and wasted fields steam
in the rising sun,
their violent ruination
grounds for a new fruition
as they become
bright gardens of winged dreams.

Water

If everything is water as the Greek said
the woman at the dhobi ghat
flapping laundry by dawn light
knows more than most
of future, past,
the living and the dead.

Hers is the articulate flute
of thaw water that runs downstream
with twigs and leaves, dead cows
and recent contamination
— E. coli, cryptosporidium —
her dream
not the white snows
of Sikkim and Tibet
but point-of-use filtration.

Which doesn't mean a bleak reductionism
since the old gods live on —
not on the high peaks
perhaps, but everywhere day breaks
on water and a washerwoman
sings to her own reflection.

Mark Rothko

Unknown adventures in an unknown space.

Bacteria drink sunlit bacteria
amid mud clouds; winds dance
and shake the rustling rice
in depths of field and hue;
the god, the divine instance,
almost reveals his hidden face.

Rough-edged, gruff, block upon block,
the great sea has gone out
leaving salt marshes, rock,
vague ripples to the horizon,
silence, colour cloud upon cloud,
brush strokes of intuition.

Red tide, rain on a twilit ocean?
God on television?
It looks dim and simple
yet is as decorative
as a Tamil temple
or Goanese baroque.

Behind the portals though
the spiritual narrative,
behind the torn veil
a rich interior glow
as of an absent presence
still desperate to get through.

Recycling Song

Swords into ploughshares, us
to birds and bushes, everyone
to topsoil in the end.
Be careful with that refuse,
respect that wrapper; once
in another life that bottle was your friend.

'What goes around . . .' The *Gita*
warns us that we never die,
something escapes the blaze.
Our smoke and methane rise
above the world of matter
in viral columns to a busy sky.

Throw nothing out; recycle
the vilest rubbish, even
your own discarded page.
Everything comes full circle:
see you again in heaven
some sunny evening in a future age.

Coco-de-Mer

So many strange species in the spice isles,
none stranger than ourselves
with our urge, evident from the word go,
to compensate for a sweaty brow
by giving stick to the slow
mule and the donkey going round.

Tired of the same springs watering the same ground,
the peace, the over-abundant choice of fruit —
crab apple, mango, guava, pomegranate
with the dew still upon it —
and desperate to escape, we found
the gates locked on the outside and a grim
rota of vigilant cherubim
to ensure we endure our fate.

It didn't happen overnight: for years
at the time of the monkey wars
our thermal images took shape
in the bright lens of a water drop,
body and soul sustained by a mute hope;
then one fine day in spring . . .

'Where art thou?' A once familiar voice
while we fret here in the evening,
the protagonists of the story.
The worm that did this thing
evicts us from our own paradise.

But still we chew on the womb-shaped *coco-de-mer*
(delicious source, goes one theory,
of our euphoria and despair),
wondering why was it planted here
in the first place
if not to tempt us into time and history.

The Great Wave

When it happened we were asleep in Bangalore
but later took a train and hired a car:
heroism or curiosity? I can't be positive
but a news instinct told us to be here.
A plate had shifted far beneath the sea
in distant Java, sending a great wave
to wreck the houses on this quiet shore.
A diffident wave breaks on the same shore

quietly this raw morning as if to say
it wouldn't hurt a fly much less destroy
a civilization, though it did just that —
hotels, schools and hospitals knocked flat
by a cliff of water smashing into the coast.
The swirling mud receded leaving a waste
of bodies, furniture, palm trunks, dereliction
and in the streets the contents of an ocean.

If 'waste is the new raw material' as they say
our resources are infinite: on black beaches
carrion, groceries, sewage, wide-open fridges
fought over by frenetic gull and crow.
Tractors haul the wreckage, dead car and cow,
balconies, splintered bits of bungalow.
On the last rock some soapstone Madurai
devotional figures . . . A post-tsunami sky.

Up at the Palace

for Anoushka Narain

Sixty-eight people died when a bomb went off
in the market place, but that was months ago.
The rest of us go on 'having our being'
in the packed streets of Jaipur, in the rough
neighbourhoods, the parks and tourist bits
of the pink city; while up at the city palace
a concert has been laid on for visitors —
ragas and Rameau under climbing stars.

The poets tell us about rooms where blind
cockroaches skitter over vile linoleum,
rats in the kitchen, scorpions in the cracks,
the Ganges choked with filth of every kind
and fog-horns mourning from the Kidderpore Docks;
but we sip champagne, we nibble the wild ducks
and follow the maharani to her pavilion
where a chamber orchestra is plucking strings.

The boy putting up posters for a pittance
and the Dalit girl-child scratching at Toyota
windows for spare change are not invited
to glitter among the balconies and arches
admiring Rajput pictures, marble elephants
and the ivory knick-knacks of the interior
but, like the crows, stare at the sumptuous
goings-on from the Govindji Temple.

The curse of karma keeps them in their places
gazing at lighted windows with rapt faces.
People, the terrible things you must have done
when you were soldiers of fortune, local kings
or naughty nautch girls in the old days!
Did you crush pearls for aphrodisiacs,

poison your cousins for a shaky throne
or cripple your tenants with a punitive tax?

No, you did nothing of the kind of course
but you were born into a dream of shame
whose violent colours filled the universe
and left you silent, each with a secret name,
listening to the music of other spheres.
You too will sip champagne one of these years
despite the old, self-perpetuating pantheon;
but what do we worship now the gods have gone?